MW01121453

/6020 1

DATE DUE	RETURNED

The
Paper
Eagle

The Paper Eagle

(Le cerf-volant)

by

Pan Bouyoucas

Translated by
Linda Gaboriau

Playwrights Canada Press
Toronto • Canada

Le cerf-volant © Copyright 1993 Pan Bouyoucas
The Paper Eagle (translation of *Le cerf-volant*) © Copyright 2006 Linda Gaboriau
The moral rights of the authors are asserted.

Playwrights Canada Press
The Canadian Drama Publisher
215 Spadina Ave. Suite 230, Toronto, Ontario CANADA M5T 2C7
416.703.0013   fax 416.408.3402
orders@playwrightscanada.com • www.playwrightscanada.com

Financial support provided by the taxpayers of Canada and Ontario through the Canada Council for the Arts, and the Department of Canadian Heritage through the Book Publishing Industry Development Programme, and the Ontario Arts Council.

Cover design: JLArt
Front cover photos © 2006 Jupiterimages Corporation
Production Editor: MZK

Library and Archives Canada Cataloguing in Publication

Bouyoucas, Pan
[Cerf-volant. English]
    Paper eagle / Pan Bouyoucas ; translated by Linda Gaboriau.

Translation of: Le Cerf-volant.

A play.

ISBN 0-88754-866-0

    I. Gaboriau, Linda II. Title.

PS8553.O89C4713 2006   C842'.54   C2006-902365-4

First edition: July 2006.
Printed and bound by AGMV at Quebec, Canada.

For my father

Translator's Note

The Greek characters in *The Paper Eagle*, like many members of Montreal's Greek community, live in a tri-lingual world. Stella, Dimitri and Andrea, now in their fifties, immigrated in their youth. At home, amongst themselves, they still speak Greek. Their children, like George now in his mid-twenties, went to French school *(la loi oblige)* and speak Québécois French, but often, if only by virtue of the neighbourhoods they live in, are drawn to speaking English.

In the original French version, to portray this linguistic potpourri, Pan Bouyoucas created three levels of French and had George (and sometimes Andrea) punctuate their conversation with occasional expressions in English. In the original, Pan established the convention that when Stella, Dimitri and Andrea speak "standard" French together, they are presumably speaking Greek. George speaks that "standard" French (i.e. Greek) to them, but punctuates it with colloquial English. Céline, the Québécoise tenant, speaks only Québécois in the original and George speaks to her in fluent, colloquial Québécois. Stella, Dimitri and Andrea attempt to speak fractured French with Céline.

Reproducing an equivalent of this linguistic potpourri in English is no easy task. In this translation of the play, I have attempted to establish the following levels of language:

When Stella, Dimitri and Andrea speak to each other in fluent, slightly "lilting" English, they are speaking Greek. When George speaks that same level of English to them, he, too, is speaking Greek. Céline speaks Québécois, but frequently lapses into English for the sake of clarity, as Québécois often do with non-French speaking people. Her English is not perfect, so I have often butchered the verb tenses or the prepositions used, etc. Dimitri and Andrea (and sometimes Stella) attempt to communicate with Céline in fractured French (as in the original version), but in this translation, they, too, lapse into English, when their vocabulary in French fails them. I have reproduced Pan Bouyoucas's phonetic transcription of their French. Their English in these speeches, unlike the English, i.e. Greek, they speak within the family, is spoken with a Greek accent, also spelled phonetically.

Lexicon

A list of Greek words and exclamations used in the English version of *Le cerf-volant*.

Diminutive and affectionate forms of characters' names:

Dimitraki (or Dimitraki *mou* = my Dimitraki)

Stellaki

Yorghaki (Yorgho = George)

Greek words or exclamations:

diávole: devil

panayítsa (mou): (my) Holy Mother

efféndi: master

ma to theó!: by God!

Thía / Thío: Aunt or Uncle

mamáka: "little" mama

ti malákas: you jerk

ástro/ástra: star / stars

omoplátes: Shoulders, upper back.

The words, *Mamá* and *Babá* (Mama and Papa) are pronounced with the accent on the last syllable.

The Paper Eagle (Le cerf-volant) was first presented by the Théâtre d'Aujourd'hui, Montreal, in February 1993 with the following company:

STELLA	Michelle Rossignol
DIMITRI	Jacques Godin
GEORGE	Emmanuel Bilodeau
ANDREA	Lionel Villeneuve
CÉLINE	Dominique Quesnel

Directed by Guy Beausoleil

Set	Daniel Castonguay
Costumes	François Laplante
Lighting	Jean-Charles Martel
Sound	Diane Lebœuf
Make-up	Angelo Barsetti
Assistant Director	Ann-Marie Corbeil
Stage Manager	Harold Bergeron

Characters

DIMITRI, a Montreal grocer of Greek origin, in his fifties.
STELLA, his wife.
GEORGE, their son, twenty-six.
ANDREA, Dimitri's older brother.
CÉLINE, Dimitri's Québécoise tenant, twenty-eight.

DIMITRI is sitting on the ground with a portable stereo, a big kite and two-thirds of a bottle of Retsina at hand. He is holding a half-empty glass of wine, staring at it distractedly, ignoring STELLA who is standing, looking at him, visibly worried.

STELLA Talk to me, Dimitri. We've always told each other everything, right? So tell me: what's the matter? Why did you come home from work? Did something happen? *(DIMITRI turns his back to her.)* Why are you turning your back on me? Are you mad at me? Now what have I done? *(DIMITRI takes a swig of wine and gargles with it.)* You having a good time? I hope you're having a good time, because from the look on your face, I'd swear you were drinking vinegar. *(DIMITRI swallows, clicking his tongue.)* At least tell me you're enjoying yourself, for God's sake! I feel like I'm going to be sick.

DIMITRI So stop talking.

STELLA Hah! You think I enjoy standing on the roof, ranting like an idiot?

DIMITRI So go back downstairs.

STELLA I'd love to, believe me, Dimitraki *mou*. I'd yodel my way back to my wash, if only I knew why you came up here.

DIMITRI I told you.

STELLA "Because it's nice and warm out today." *(DIMITRI takes out a pack of cigarettes.)* You left work in the middle of the day because it's nice and warm—

DIMITRI I've got the right!

STELLA Not when you're the boss.

DIMITRI What a stupid thing to say. Now I can't take time off because I'm the boss!

STELLA That's what you've always said yourself.

DIMITRI   I changed my mind.

He takes a carrot stick out of the cigarette pack.

STELLA   You changed your mind...

DIMITRI   Yes.

STELLA   Just like that, the day of the big specials.

DIMITRI   There are specials every goddamn day of the week.

He takes a bite of his carrot stick. STELLA glances at her watch.

STELLA   You're right. You deserve a rest. The kids are grown up, the house is paid for, you can sell your business and take it easy for the rest of your life. What do you say? Would you like that? *(DIMITRI pushes a button on the portable stereo: Greek music.)* Okay, okay, I'll leave. You don't have to make a scene. *(She leans over to lower the music.)* Your sister's probably spread the word to every Greek in the neighbourhood. No sense in bringing all the *Québécois* up on the rooftops too. You know they hate being reminded that we exist.

DIMITRI   That's a fact.

He drinks his wine. STELLA caresses his head.

STELLA   What's the matter? *(DIMITRI stands up, swearing.)* Dimitri, put yourself in my place. You come back from an errand and someone tells you that your wife, the wife you thought was at work, is up on the roof guzzling retsina. What would you do, eh? Bring me up a deck chair and a bowl of pistachios? We've been married for twenty-eight years. Since when do you drink during the day, except on Sundays? We've been living in this house for twenty-five years. Have you ever been on the roof before? Answer me, maybe I forgot... *(DIMITRI takes another bite of his carrot.)* ANSWER ME!

DIMITRI   You don't have to yell...

STELLA has tears in her eyes. DIMITRI looks at her, ill at ease.

STELLA   You're sick! Is that why you stopped smoking? I've been asking you to give it up for years, how come you decided to stop now? We could count the number of times you've listened to me on one hand. So why did you suddenly stop? Tell me. At this point, I'm prepared for anything. You've got cancer...

DIMITRI   It won't be long.

STELLA   Dimitri, I don't feel like joking.

DIMITRI   Keep it up and I will have cancer: cancer of the eardrums.

STELLA   Don't worry. If anyone around here's going to get it, it'll be me. Cancer of the throat. If I don't have it already.

DIMITRI   Congratulations. You've been talking about it for so long—

STELLA   Take that back! *(She crosses herself.)* Stop walking around! It's making me dizzy!

DIMITRI   So go back downstairs! Leave me alone!

STELLA   Alright, alright, come sit down and I'll leave. Dimitri, please! Don't go so close to the edge. I had a bad dream last night. Come sit down. I'm leaving. *(She looks at her watch, stalls, while DIMITRI sits down. She speaks to herself.)* Where the hell is he?

DIMITRI   So, what are you waiting for?

STELLA   Okay, okay, I've got errands to do. It's your nephew's birthday tomorrow and I still haven't bought him a present.... Do you think he'd like a kite?

DIMITRI   He'll know once he has one.

STELLA	That's true. How much are they?
DIMITRI	Twenty dollars.
STELLA	Oh, that's not so bad. You want to drive me? Since you've got the day off. I can't drag a kite around in the bus.
DIMITRI	I'll go pick one out myself later on.

He turns his back to her. Beat.

STELLA	There's some chicken left over from yesterday... *(No response from DIMITRI.)* Too many hormones in chicken.... How about some feta and olives? *(No response.)* Have you stopped eating too? Tell me if you're on a diet. You think I enjoy spending my mornings scooping out zucchini and my afternoons stuffing them? *(DIMITRI raises his glass and sighs.)* Dimitri, you shouldn't drink on an empty stomach.
DIMITRI	Leave me alone!
STELLA	Especially on a roof...
DIMITRI	I've eaten!
STELLA	You sure don't look like you have. You've got circles down to your bellybutton.
DIMITRI	I haven't slept for three days!
STELLA	You haven't slept for three days?
DIMITRI	Why did I say that! *(He stands up.)*
STELLA	Why didn't you tell me?
DIMITRI	There's nothing to tell.
STELLA	There must be a reason.
DIMITRI	Don't you ever have trouble sleeping?
STELLA	Every other night.
DIMITRI	So...

STELLA	So what?
DIMITRI	So you should understand.
STELLA	No, I'm not psychic like you, I can't guess what's worrying other people. So tell me: why are you having trouble sleeping?
DIMITRI	*(looking at her)* Don't you have something on the stove?
STELLA	No. Why? Do you smell something burning?
DIMITRI	Impossible. You've always got something on the stove.
STELLA	I haven't started supper yet. We're out of potatoes. I asked you to bring some home yesterday…
DIMITRI	I forgot.
STELLA	And the day before yesterday…
DIMITRI	Alright, alright! I forgot! It happens.
STELLA	There are too many strange things happening all of a sudden. If you were twenty, I'd swear you were in love.
DIMITRI	But at my age I'm more likely to have cancer, right?

> *He walks over to the edge of the roof and stares off into the distance. We can hear a siren in the distance. STELLA goes over to DIMITRI.*

STELLA	Dimitri… *(He walks away from her again.)* Will you stand still! You're making me dizzy. *(Ignoring her, DIMITRI walks to the far end of the roof. We can hear the siren coming closer.)* Great! Somebody must've called for the straitjackets!
DIMITRI	I hope so.
STELLA	Stop talking like that! It's bad luck. *(She crosses herself.)*

DIMITRI   You can cross yourself with your feet too, Stella, it won't change a thing. All your amulets, your icons and your prayers can't change a thing. Sooner or later, we all have to go for a ride in an ambulance. All of us. And you're right, our turn is coming up. It won't be long. And I intend to keep my eyes wide open so I can appreciate every minute. *(He bites into his carrot stick. The siren is moving away from the house.)* Too bad. Looks like my turn hasn't come yet.

          He spits his carrot stick over the side of the roof and picks up his wine glass. STELLA is watching him, increasingly worried. DIMITRI drinks his last mouthful of wine, gargling with it before swallowing, then leans over to refill his glass. This time STELLA stops him by grabbing his arm.

STELLA   Come downstairs with me. I can't go down alone, it gives me vertigo.

DIMITRI   You came up here on your own.

STELLA   I can't see the drop on my way up…

DIMITRI   I guess nobody in this goddamn house can get along without me! *(He puts his glass down on the ground.)* Okay, let's go. *(STELLA picks up the bottle.)* What do you think you're doing?

STELLA   You shouldn't leave wine in the sun. You can come back up after your nap.

DIMITRI   I don't want to take a nap!

STELLA   If you haven't slept for three days…

DIMITRI   Stella!

STELLA   Just fifteen minutes…

DIMITRI   Stella, I swear on my father's grave, if you don't give that bottle back to me, I'm going to go down and piss on your icons!

STELLA	Shut up, *diavole*. Forgive him, *panayitsa mou*, it's the wine. He's not used to drinking in the sun. *(DIMITRI yanks the bottle away from her. STELLA looks around hastily.)* Good thing nobody's watching us, otherwise I wouldn't dare show my face in the neighbourhood. *(DIMITRI sits down and fills his glass.)* Why are you doing this? If you want to go for a ride in an ambulance, I'll rent one for you. You don't have to fall off the roof.

GEORGE appears.

GEORGE	You two need an audience now?
STELLA	Ha! It's about time you showed up.
GEORGE	Everyone can hear you from the street!
STELLA	What took you so long? Were you waiting for us to fall?
GEORGE	Great idea! *(He turns to leave.)* Then I can come around to collect the rent, instead of the usual reproaches.
STELLA	All right, I'll shut up. Go talk to your father. I won't say a thing. You talk to him, because I'm starting to get blisters on my tongue.

DIMITRI stands up, offended.

DIMITRI	You sure you don't have blisters on your brain?
GEORGE	Don't start yelling again!
DIMITRI	*(as he walks away from them)* Poor woman! She gets her son to come over, as if I was senile!
STELLA	*(to DIMITRI)* I suppose you find it normal for a fifty-five-year-old man to leave work so he can fly a kite on the roof of his house?
GEORGE	Fly a what?
STELLA	A kite. *(pointing to the kite lying on the roof)* Look!

GEORGE   Wow! Neat! It's a beauty.

         DIMITRI glances at GEORGE—at last someone shares his taste.

STELLA   Is that all you've got to say?

GEORGE   Don't you think it's beautiful? *(to DIMITRI)* I didn't know you liked kites. *(He picks up the kite.)* It must have cost at least a hundred dollars.

STELLA   A hundred...?

DIMITRI   *(avoiding the subject)* Give it to me. You're going to tear it.

         He grabs the kite and walks off, his finger in the air, testing the wind.

STELLA   A hundred dollars!

GEORGE   Is it a full moon tonight?

STELLA   Why? You've got to go howl on top of Mount Royal?

GEORGE   Jesus!

STELLA   I wouldn't be at all surprised. You'd rather spend the evening with a skunk than with your own mother.

GEORGE   Don't take your bad mood out on me again, okay?

STELLA   Fine, fine. Did anything happen to him?

GEORGE   How should I know? He never talks to me about anything personal. Call his brother.

STELLA   I already did. He hasn't talked to him either.

GEORGE   What's the big deal, anyway? So, he's not the type who leaves work to fly a kite. That doesn't mean that he's going to start eating his own caca.

STELLA   It's not just the kite. He won't stop drinking. What will I do if he falls? He's the only one I can count on, come rain or shine. Because my son, ever since he's tasted other breasts, he's forgotten the ones that fed him.

GEORGE   (*glancing around*) God, I hope no one heard you.

STELLA   What are you waiting for? Get him off the roof before he falls.

GEORGE   You think he'll listen to me?!

STELLA   Try. Pretend he's some blonde you're trying to get into bed.

GEORGE   Maybe it's the full moon. Maybe it's his menopause…

STELLA   What are you talking about?

GEORGE   Men go through menopause too.

STELLA   And do they start hallucinating and talking to spiders?

> DIMITRI, *who was walking by, his finger in the air to test the wind, overhears her.*

DIMITRI   I talk to spiders?

STELLA   He's starting to lose his memory too!

GEORGE   What are you talking about? What spiders?

STELLA   (*to DIMITRI*) Last night weren't you watching a spider walk between your feet?

DIMITRI   I don't have the right to do that either?

STELLA   Why didn't you kill it, the pretty little spider?

DIMITRI   Why should I have killed it?

STELLA   Oh, sorry, *effendi*! That was the maid's job. Excuse me.

DIMITRI   But I didn't want you to kill it!

STELLA   Why not, Dimitraki? So you could whisper more sweet nothings to it?

DIMITRI   Go ahead, tell him you think I'm soft in the head!

GEORGE   Stop, both of you! We're on a rooftop. Don't you realize that, you goddamn peasants? You're on a rooftop… in Montreal…! Now. Let's start all over. There was a spider on the floor…

DIMITRI   And I was watching it…

STELLA   In the middle of the news.

GEORGE   Will you let him finish!

STELLA   Usually he doesn't blink an eye during the news.

DIMITRI   I'm going to strangle her, *ma to theó*, I'm going to strangle her!

GEORGE   Not so loud!

DIMITRI   What about her? Why always me? Can't you hear her?

STELLA   Alright, alright, I won't say a thing. Go ahead, tell him. I won't open my mouth even if they come to tell me I just won the 6/49.

GEORGE   *Mamá! (STELLA seals her lips.)* So. You were watching a spider…

DIMITRI   Yeah. And while I was looking at it, I wondered— maybe I said it out loud, I don't know—but I just wondered if spiders know that we exist. Us humans.

GEORGE   If spiders know that we exist… I've never thought about it. I don't think so. Unless we step on them…?

DIMITRI   Even if we step on them…

GEORGE   You're right, then it's too late.

STELLA   I knew it! It's hereditary!

GEORGE   I really don't see what's wrong with asking yourself questions like that. In fact, I'm surprised, pleasantly surprised, to see that my father asks himself that kind of question.

DIMITRI   *(to STELLA)* Ha!

STELLA   *(to GEORGE) En français?*

DIMITRI   *En français?*

STELLA   Yes. Now you can be really proud of your *"papa."* Not only does he discuss philosophy with spiders, he now yells at me *en français.*

DIMITRI   Who me?

STELLA   You didn't yell at me last night?

DIMITRI   Because you killed the spider. But not in French.

STELLA   Now he doesn't remember that either!

DIMITRI   Why would I yell at you in French? You can hardly speak the language.

STELLA   Ask your sister.

DIMITRI   She wasn't here yesterday! Enough is enough! If you're looking for an excuse to have me locked up, find something better!

STELLA   I'm talking about Sunday. Was your sister here on Sunday or not?

GEORGE   What happened on Sunday?

STELLA   For the past twenty-eight years, we've been taking our Sunday afternoon walk together, right? Well now, *Monsieur* doesn't want me to go with him any more. And when I insisted last Sunday, he started yelling at me!

GEORGE   *(trying not to laugh) En français?*

STELLA   You find that funny?

DIMITRI   *(trying to remember)* That's crazy. Why would I yell in French? I don't speak it any better than you do.

STELLA   Call your sister. She's probably hiding over there on her roof, stalking a crisis like a vampire stalks a throat. Go ahead. Yell to her, from one roof to another. It'll remind you of your beautiful mountains. You bunch of hicks.

DIMITRI Oh, go—

STELLA Go ahead, say it. You've been dying to say it for a month. I can tell. I can feel it—

GEORGE *Mamá*, stop!

STELLA ...Go ahead. Tell me to go to the edge of the roof and make like a birdie.

GEORGE Stop it, both of you. Stop or I'm leaving. *(DIMITRI walks away from them, swearing.)* Why don't you get off his back? If he's sick...

STELLA All the more reason. If somebody swallowed a bottle of sleeping pills, what would you do, let them sleep? Don't answer. You probably would. Just look at you... you've got circles down to your knees.

GEORGE Here we go again.

STELLA A good-looking boy like you. What a waste. Show me your tongue.

GEORGE Jesus, Ma! Will you get off my case!

STELLA Okay, okay. I'll fix you a steak, but first tell him to get off the roof, because I'm—

GEORGE You're about to get cancer.

STELLA That's it, laugh. Just wait until I get it, then we'll see who has the last laugh.

GEORGE Do you realize what you just said?

STELLA No, I don't know what I'm saying anymore. You've all managed to scramble my brains. You and your tofu and your infantile dabbling—

GEORGE They're paintings! Paintings!

STELLA   …your sister who starts choking every time
                I mention the word marriage. And now the old
                man who's taken to playing on the rooftops!

GEORGE   Big deal. For once in his life…

STELLA   Oh, sure. I wonder how you'd react if it was me,
                eh? Go over there and talk to him. Go ahead, before
                I start ranting and raving *en français*. Hurry up, I get
                dizzy just standing on a stepladder.

GEORGE   So go downstairs.

STELLA   By myself?

GEORGE   I'll help you.

STELLA   And leave him on his own? I know there's not much
                more he can give you and your sister before he's
                dead and buried. But if you don't mind, I'd like to
                keep him so I can appreciate him a bit longer. Even if
                all you've left me is his skin and bones. He's the only
                person on this earth who understands me and who
                I can understand. Look, what did I tell you!

GEORGE   What?

STELLA   Radio Montreal!

GEORGE   Ah! *(loudly)* Hello, *Thía* Sophia!

STELLA   Don't tell me you're going to start yelling from the
                rooftops like them! *(under her breath, as she waves to
                her sister-in-law)* Go talk to him! *(GEORGE goes to join
                his father. To her sister-in-law.)* He just came home to
                show his son how to fly a kite. *(to herself)* Why don't
                they get vertigo? *(to her sister-in-law)* Of course, I'd
                be glad to ask him. If the Québec tomatoes have
                arrived, I want some too. *(to herself)* Must come
                from their childhood, chasing after their goats in the
                mountains. *(to her sister-in-law)* You're right, I am
                spoiled. My Dimitri would bring me bird's milk if
                I asked him to. *(to herself)* Now look at me, yelling
                on the rooftops like a peasant! *(waves goodbye to her*

sister-in-law) Bye now! See you later. *(to herself)* Go ahead. Run and call your sisters-in-law in Park Ex and your cousins in Laval!

DIMITRI   *(refusing to listen to GEORGE)* No, no!

GEORGE   There's no wind…

DIMITRI   There will be. They said so on the radio.

GEORGE   Let's go wait for it in the park.

DIMITRI   You want people to laugh at me?

GEORGE   You don't think you look funny on the roof?

DIMITRI   This is my roof and the space over my roof is mine too!

GEORGE   But don't you need more space lengthwise? To run and get that thing into the air?

DIMITRI   I've got enough. I should know. I paid for it, inch by inch, with the best years of my life.

GEORGE   And what if you start running and you can't stop at the edge?

DIMITRI   I won't fall.

GEORGE   *Babá…*

DIMITRI   I won't fall! I know what I'm doing. This isn't the first time I've flown a kite.

GEORGE   Oh, really? You do it at night? As far as I can remember, during the daytime, you never even had time to teach me the word for kite.

DIMITRI   *(looking at his son)* Do you remember the last time I wanted to play ball with you in the park?

GEORGE   No.

DIMITRI   Well, I remember. I could play with you as long as I spoke English.

GEORGE	I was ten years old.
DIMITRI	I wasn't.

He walks off, holding his finger in the air. STELLA comes over to GEORGE.

STELLA	So?
GEORGE	So what?
STELLA	What did he say?

Suddenly we hear Charles Dumont singing his lungs out in the flat below them.

DIMITRI Well, well, our little love-bunnies finally woke up... Just in time to have supper and start screwing again! *(He puts his kite down on the roof.)*

GEORGE *(to STELLA)* Who's he talking about?

STELLA What are you talking about?

DIMITRI Can't you hear it?

STELLA The music?

DIMITRI Not just the music! Can't you hear them at night? Creak, creak, creak, right over our bed! I can even hear them at the store! No wonder it takes them all day to recover!

He picks up the stereo and turns on the Greek music full blast.

GEORGE What the hell are you doing?

DIMITRI Making noise!

GEORGE Why now? If you wanted to disturb them, you should've done it while they were trying to sleep.

DIMITRI doesn't answer, he's too busy jumping on the roof. Instinctively, his feet follow the beat of the Greek music.

STELLA   Dimitri! You're going to make a hole in the roof!

DIMITRI   I don't give a damn.

STELLA   Don't say that...

DIMITRI   I hope the whole goddamn house comes tumbling down and buries me alive!

STELLA   Stop! It hurts me to hear you say that.

DIMITRI   I don't give a good goddamn.

GEORGE   I'm leaving.

STELLA   No! Don't leave me alone with him!

GEORGE   Why not, the two of you understand each other so well...

STELLA   Oh no! I think I'm going to faint.

> *DIMITRI is kneeling at the edge of the roof, swinging his stereo over the side. His music has completely drowned out Charles Dumont.*

GEORGE   Hey! Are you crazy?

> *He wants to go stop his father, but STELLA holds him back.*

STELLA   No!

GEORGE   Don't worry, I don't get vertigo.

STELLA   Yes, you do! You're not like them...

GEORGE   *Mamá...*

STELLA   ...You're an Athenian! Like me!

GEORGE   *Mamá*, don't start that crap again, let go of me!

STELLA   No! Let him fall! If he's tired of living, let him fall! But he's not taking my child with him!

> *ANDREA appears on the roof. He motions to them to remain silent and tiptoes over to DIMITRI. In*

one swift move, he grabs him by the collar and pulls him over onto his back.

ANDREA   Is this what happens when a guy smokes carrots?

STELLA's nerves finally give and she starts kicking and yelling at DIMITRI.

STELLA   You donkey! Crazy fool! Neurotic!

GEORGE   *(trying to control her)* Mamá! Stop!

STELLA   My father was right! He said you were a barbarian. But I wouldn't listen. Now I wonder why, you damn peasant!

GEORGE   Stop!

STELLA   I wonder what I ever saw in you!

GEORGE   Think of what the neighbours are going to say!

ANDREA stops the music. Silence. Even Charles Dumont has stopped singing, but nobody notices.

DIMITRI   Poor Dimitri. You give them everything you've got, and they pay you back with kicks. What's next?

ANDREA   C'mon, you don't have to turn it into a tragedy. Stand up.

DIMITRI   I just wanted to sit in the sun for a while. Spring went by before I knew it, and summer's almost over. After all I've done for them, don't I even have the right to spend an afternoon in the sun before winter hits us over the head again? *(He stands up.)*

ANDREA   Why on the roof? You've got a backyard…

DIMITRI   Have you come to tell me what to do, too?

ANDREA   You don't have to yell.

GEORGE   He doesn't know any better. And he wonders why I spent my childhood trying to hide my parents from my friends.

DIMITRI   Will he ever get off my back! Go ahead, take your *mamaka*'s side, ungrateful brat, but just get off my back! All of you! Do I have to spell it out? I look at you, and I think I'm going to suffocate. So get out of here! I've got the right to be alone! This is my roof! So scram! *(He picks up his glass of wine.)*

ANDREA   *(to the others)* Go downstairs.

DIMITRI   You go too. I don't need anybody.

> *He takes a sip of his wine. ANDREA gestures to the others to leave.*

STELLA   *(whispering)* I can't leave him, Andrea. He's suffering.

ANDREA   *(whispering)* No, no...

STELLA   *(whispering)* He's never spoken to me like that before, never.

ANDREA   *(whispering)* I'll take care of him. Leave us alone.

> *Charles Dumont starts singing again. DIMITRI puts his glass down, swearing, but GEORGE beats him to the stereo.*

DIMITRI   Give that to me.

GEORGE   I'll talk to her. Just relax, okay? I'll go tell her to turn her music down.

DIMITRI   No! Music or no music, I want her out of here!

ANDREA   *(to STELLA)* Who's he talking about?

DIMITRI   Tell her she's got twenty-four hours to vacate the premises.

STELLA   The new tenant.

DIMITRI   *(to GEORGE)* Why are you looking at me like that, Yorghaki? Do I have to say it in English?

GEORGE   You want to kick her out because she made the floor creak one night?

DIMITRI   Three nights!

STELLA   Well, well...

DIMITRI   And I'd tell her myself if I spoke French better!

STELLA   You'd tell her what?

GEORGE   Think about it. What would you tell her?

DIMITRI   To pack up her jolly jumper and get the hell out of here. I rented that flat to one person. One. I didn't rent it so they could turn it into a bordello.

GEORGE   C'mon, she's got a right to bring a guy home with her.

DIMITRI   Absolutely. But not so she can be his trampoline right over my head every night. I want to sleep. You hear me? I want to sleep! And I'm not going to wear earplugs in my own house!

STELLA   So tell her to change bedrooms.

GEORGE   Right—

DIMITRI   Forget it. I'll go myself.

GEORGE   No! The state you're in, you might punch her in the face.

STELLA   Let him go. It's about time he discovered that not all women are pushovers like me.

DIMITRI   You, a pushover?

GEORGE   Here we go again!

DIMITRI   Did you hear what she said? Because he was born an angel, Lucifer tries to make us believe he's angelic.

STELLA   And I suppose you're the Good Lord himself?

GEORGE   You know what? You two deserve each other. Honestly, you really deserve each other.

STELLA   Maybe. Maybe I do deserve him. But I'd like to know why. I'd like to know what I did to the Virgin Mary to deserve the pain that's clawing at my heart this very minute. *(She looks at DIMITRI.)* I was prepared for just about anything from you, but not this. Not this.

DIMITRI   You weren't prepared for what?

> *STELLA is already headed towards the way down from the roof.*

GEORGE   Wait. Don't go down alone. *(to DIMITRI)* I'll go talk to the girl. Okay? Calm down. I'm on my way.

> *GEORGE exits with his mother. DIMITRI stares at the exit.*

DIMITRI   What wasn't she prepared for? She hits me in front of my own son and my brother, and I'm the one who's supposed to feel guilty?

> *ANDREA takes out a pack of cigarettes.*

ANDREA   Here, have one.

DIMITRI   I quit.

ANDREA   I know.

DIMITRI   I wonder why. To spare my health so I can work, work so I can eat, eat to stay alive, so I can go on working...

ANDREA   If you're fed up with the store, sell it.

DIMITRI   It's not the store. The store's allowed me to feed my family, buy a house, give my kids an education. I'll never dump on that. It's not the store.

ANDREA   So what is it?

DIMITRI   You wouldn't understand.

ANDREA   Try me. I have my moments of lucidity. What's bugging you?

DIMITRI   ...Silence.

ANDREA   Huh?

DIMITRI   Can't you hear it? Silence, at last! *(Charles Dumont has stopped singing. DIMITRI takes out a carrot stick, taps it on the pack, like a cigarette.)* I'll show her! She can threaten to immolate herself on my doorstep and I'll still slam the door in her face!

ANDREA   What have you got against her? What did she do to you?

DIMITRI   Weren't you listening?

ANDREA   Mitso, we're alone now. Have a real cigarette and tell me...

DIMITRI   Will you stop bugging me with your goddamn cigarettes! Why do you all think I mean black when I say white? When I say, No, I'm not going to smoke any more, it's no. I'm no slave to my habits! *(He takes a bite of his carrot.)* Hey, a bit of wind! *(He raises his kite.)*

ANDREA   Will you put that thing down so we can talk like grownups, man-to-man, for a minute. *(DIMITRI ignores him and starts pacing up and down the roof, holding his index finger in the air. ANDREA changes his approach.)* What a pretty kite. I've never seen such a nice one in the stores. Where did you find it?

DIMITRI   Down in Old Montreal. Do you remember?

ANDREA   What?

DIMITRI   The kite we made when we were kids.

ANDREA   Bah...

DIMITRI   Honestly!

ANDREA   What do you expect me to say? Yes, I remember our kite—it was pathetic.

DIMITRI   You're pathetic.

ANDREA   Well, wasn't it pathetic compared to this one?

DIMITRI   That's not the point. *(He lowers his finger.)* Strange, I thought I felt a gust of wind.

ANDREA   What were you doing in Old Montreal?

DIMITRI   I felt like having a coffee in the sun. It was cold in the store. Probably the lack of sleep. And outside... it looked so warm outside. *(He puts down the kite.)* Do you realize that I've spent thirty summers in Montreal and I had never set foot in a *café-terrasse*. I'm at the store when the sun rises in Halifax, and I'm still at the store when the sun sets in Vancouver.

ANDREA   My restaurant has a *terrasse*...

DIMITRI   I didn't feel like smelling souvlaki and listening to your employees' dumb jokes. I didn't even feel like having a coffee. I just wanted to sit in the sun and look at something besides old ladies squeezing the eggplants. *(He takes out another carrot stick.)*

ANDREA   So?

DIMITRI   So what?

ANDREA   So, how were the young ladies squeezing the cappucinos?

DIMITRI   Nothing to write home about.

ANDREA   What did you expect?

DIMITRI   I don't know, something, anything. For once I'd left the store... I even ordered my coffee in English, just to see...

ANDREA   To see what?

DIMITRI   If the waitress would say anything.

ANDREA   So? What happened?

DIMITRI   Nothing. It was.... It was like I wasn't even there. As if I didn't exist... *(He takes a bite of his carrot.)*

ANDREA	You should have gone to the corner of St. Lawrence and St. Catherine.
DIMITRI	There's no *café-terrasse*—
ANDREA	No, but if you wanted some girl to notice you—
DIMITRI	Did I say that?
ANDREA	Don't get mad—
DIMITRI	Why do you have to degrade everything? Ach, I don't know why I even told you. You don't understand anything—
ANDREA	Maybe—
DIMITRI	No, you don't. All you understand is money or a piece of ass.
ANDREA	That's true.
DIMITRI	And the worst of it is, when someone tries to talk to you about feelings, you treat him like an idiot…
ANDREA	Or a hypocrite.
DIMITRI	So you admit it.
ANDREA	I never tried to hide it.
DIMITRI	Don't you make yourself sick?
ANDREA	Often.

DIMITRI *looks at* ANDREA *suspiciously.*

DIMITRI	Why are you agreeing with me?
ANDREA	Because you're right.
DIMITRI	I've always been right on that subject. So why do you suddenly agree with me? What's going on in the back of your mind?
ANDREA	Now who's acting suspicious? I'm just saying that you're right. I, your older brother, admit that I'm wrong…

DIMITRI   Okay, forget it…

ANDREA   You shit all over me and you dare talk about
            feelings?!

DIMITRI   Okay! I'm… I'm… *(He clears his throat.)* Goddamn
            carrots! You want some wine?

ANDREA   No, I've got to go back to work.

DIMITRI   Work, work… *(He lifts his glass and sniffs the Retsina.)*
            I drank my coffee, then I went for a little drive
            through Old Montreal. That's when I spotted the kite
            store. A whole window full of them, big ones, little
            ones, red, yellow…. They even had heart-shaped
            ones. Anyway, I parked out front and looked at them
            for at least an hour. You can't imagine all the sights,
            all the smells and sounds it brought back. I swear,
            I was sitting there staring at them and at one point
            I thought I heard the *Saturnia*'s siren.

ANDREA   Whose siren?

DIMITRI   The *Saturnia*'s, the boat that brought us to Canada.

ANDREA   You were right next to the harbour, dummy.

DIMITRI   Maybe, but… I could've sworn it was the *Saturnia*.
            How could I ever forget it? It was the first boat siren
            I'd ever heard. And the last…

ANDREA   Thank God.

DIMITRI   Why?

ANDREA   Can you see us taking the boat again at our age?
            Even at twenty, you never fully recover from a heart
            transplant.

DIMITRI   Do you remember what we told each other, down in
            our cabin trying to forget how seasick we were?
            We'll go here, we'll go there, we'll see this, we'll do
            that…. Where have we gone, Andrea? What have we
            seen, besides home and work? What have we done?
            Just long enough to learn a few words, to get used to

walking in the snow, to build a little security and it's already time to pack up and leave on the big trip.... Sometimes... Sometimes I wonder if we shouldn't have stayed in Greece. They're not starving over there. And in the cafés, we'd understand what people were laughing about, and people would understand what we were sighing about...

ANDREA   Don't you think it's a bit silly making our hearts sigh at our age?

DIMITRI   You should see my tenant's boyfriend. *(He empties his glass.)*

ANDREA   Why, is he old?

DIMITRI   Yeah, but he's *Québécois.*

ANDREA   What's that supposed to mean?

DIMITRI   That means that when he opens his eyes in the morning, he can dream about something other than *le Festival du broccoli. (He pulls a carrot stick out of his pack.)*

ANDREA   Must be quite a looker.

DIMITRI   No, he's not even good-looking.

ANDREA   I'm talking about this tenant who makes old men sigh.

DIMITRI   You've got sex on the brain!

ANDREA   Don't have to be a genius...

DIMITRI   I'm talking about dreams, you ignoramus! The kind of dreams that used to help us face anything, the kind we don't have anymore.

ANDREA   And never will have again.

DIMITRI   Don't say that.

ANDREA   Mitso...

DIMITRI   I swear, if I thought that all I had to look forward to was the store during the day and the TV at night, I'd throw myself off the roof right this minute.

ANDREA   Come off it, will you? What's gotten into you all of a sudden? *(He takes him by the shoulders.)* Listen. Sometimes I feel that way too…. Are you listening to me?

DIMITRI   Yeah, yeah.

ANDREA   Sometimes when I hear them talking in my restaurant and I don't understand half of what they're saying, sometimes I feel like I don't exist too. So I think about Alexander.

DIMITRI   You think about your son?!

ANDREA   The Great, you moron. Alexander the Great.

DIMITRI   Standing there behind your counter, you think about Alexander the Great…

ANDREA   Right. Did Alexander speak Persian when he set out to conquer Persia?

DIMITRI   What bullshit profundity is he going to come out with next!

ANDREA   I'm talking about the Gordian knot, dummy! The knot we had to untie if we wanted to rule Asia. And what did he do, Alexander? Fast—because he was running out of time too—he pulled out his sword and slash…! I know, we're not in Babylon anymore. But we've got other ways of slashing knots.

           He opens his wallet and lets his collection of credit cards unfold.

DIMITRI   Twenty billion—

ANDREA   Not quite.

DIMITRI   Twenty billion years—the Big Bang, the formation of the Milky Way, the solar system, the planet Earth, forty thousand generations in the evolution of the species—and it's come to this! Do you know what you are?

ANDREA   You've already told me.

DIMITRI   You're a misanthrope.

ANDREA   Ah ha! That's new!

DIMITRI   Admit it. You must despise people to treat them the way you do.

ANDREA   Let's just say I find them funny. Sometimes they can be really funny. Look at yourself.

DIMITRI   You make me sick.

ANDREA   Is that going to help you sleep any better tonight?

DIMITRI   You'll never change.

ANDREA   Knock on wood.

DIMITRI   My father was right. He was right when he used to say—but I bet you've forgotten that too—

ANDREA   What? He came out with so many gems, our Yorgho the Great...

DIMITRI   "The more you have between the legs, the less you have between the ears!"

ANDREA   What's with this obsession anyway, why do you frustrated, unhappy people need to make happy people feel guilty? Why, eh? To justify your lack of guts? Poor bastard! Why do we break our backs all our lives—you, me, everyone—if it isn't for the almighty dollar? And what's the dollar, if it isn't the power to untie knots?

DIMITRI   If dumb ideas were feathers, Andrea, you would have flown away ages ago.

ANDREA   They might be dumb ideas—

DIMITRI   Sometimes—

ANDREA —but I'm not the one who's shouting from the rooftops!

DIMITRI I'm telling you, sometimes, I can't believe we came from the same womb.

ANDREA And from the same seed. Say it. From the same idealistic father who believed that he could change the world by waving a red rag.

DIMITRI It wasn't a rag! It was a dream!

ANDREA Yeah, yeah. "Bread and justice."

DIMITRI That's right! The kind of dream you've never had and never will have!

ANDREA "Bread and justice for all!" I can still hear him, especially lately when I watch the news and see what's become of his famous Lenin's dream. "Bread and justice for all." Bullshit! His wife and kids got lots of both, thanks to his dream. Maybe when you look back, all you see is a Prometheus who could bring water to a boil just staring at it, and the pathetic kite we once made in order to forget our misery. But me, I see myself at twelve picking tobacco leaves from sunrise to sunset so we could buy a loaf of bread. Because our saviour preferred to get himself shot rather than let go of his dream! Well now, when his wife wants a loaf of bread, I can buy her a bakery. And you can dump on me all you want, I'll never regret what I had to do to get this far. Just seeing the way my kids and my grandchildren smile at me when I arrive with my arms full of goodies is all the reward I need. And if I feel like stroking some silky, young thighs, I buy myself that pleasure. Yes, I prefer to buy it, instead of going on the warpath, like the old man used to do, and like you're doing right now to make your dream come true!

DIMITRI What the hell are you talking about? What dream? What warpath?

ANDREA   I'm talking about you and your threat to close down
           your tenant's bordello if she doesn't invite old
           Greeks too.

DIMITRI   You think that I—

ANDREA   Mitso, when a man suffocates in the shade and
           shivers in the sun, he's not suffering from a lack of
           sleep.

DIMITRI   In my wife's house!

ANDREA   Wake up, you're going to be in your wife's house till
           the day you die. And there's no ass once you're six
           feet under. No ass, no wine, no jasmine, no nothing.
           And the only principles that count there are those of
           the worms.

DIMITRI   I bet you can hardly wait to be buried, eh?

ANDREA   Don't be nasty, I'm trying to help you—

DIMITRI   I don't need anybody's help, especially yours. Get
           lost.

ANDREA   Mitso—

DIMITRI   Get out of here! *(He throws his carrot in ANDREA's
           face.)* Think of all the souvlakis you could be selling
           right now and all the silky thighs you could buy
           with those dollars! Get out of my house!

ANDREA   *(hurt)* You're a great guy, Dimitri. More than
           a brother. But sometimes you act like a real asshole.

DIMITRI   We'll see. *(He picks up the bottle.)* We'll see if it's just
           an empty threat. *(He takes a swig.)*

ANDREA   Mitso, don't do anything stupid just to prove me
           wrong. *(DIMITRI gargles.)* Bastard. You're nothing
           but a lousy phony, just like the old man...! Look at
           yourself, you stupid ass! And look at me! What am
           I supposed to do? I'm fifty-seven, I'm an immigrant.
           I'm not an M.P. or a movie star. I'm no ladykiller, so
           what you do expect me to do? Cut off my balls? *(He*

sees STELLA reappear and changes his tone.) I swear to you, someday, I'm going to do it. When I no longer need them, I'll get myself castrated and I'll mail them in with my tax return. Maybe then they'll understand what they're doing to us.

STELLA   Poor Andrea. They've discovered more undeclared income?

ANDREA   No, we're talking about the new taxes.

> *STELLA is holding a tray with four cups of Greek coffee and three plates of baklava.*

DIMITRI   Why don't you bring up the Hibachi too, and we'll invite the whole neighbourhood over.

STELLA   I'm doing this for you, so you don't look so crazy. You want kids to start making faces at you in the street? Here, Andrea…

DIMITRI   No, he's leaving.

ANDREA   I always have time when my sister-in-law offers me a coffee. *(to STELLA, as he takes a cup)* Will you read my grounds afterwards?

STELLA   Of course. Sit down, and have a baklava.

ANDREA   No, thanks. I just had a carrot.

> *He lights a cigarette. DIMITRI looks daggers at him. As his wife passes him a plate with a piece of baklava he asks her.*

DIMITRI   Did he tell her to vacate the premises?

STELLA   I don't know. *(She puts down the tray.)*

DIMITRI   Is he still in her flat?

STELLA   He's not in ours.

DIMITRI   I should have gone myself. He gets a hard-on just watching girls walk down the street. If she greets him lounging on her sofa in her short shorts, he's

	capable of betraying his own father. *(He goes to the edge of the roof and yells downstairs.)* One son. I only have one son, and he had to turn out like his uncle!
STELLA	Dimitri! Don't start that again! *(DIMITRI walks back towards them, stamping his feet.)* Enough!
DIMITRI	*(to ANDREA)* Haven't you finished your coffee yet?
STELLA	Why are you taking it out on him now?

DIMITRI takes a cup of coffee and walks away without answering. He starts pacing up and down the roof, stopping now and then to stamp his feet.

ANDREA	Don't worry. He's not planning to jump.
STELLA	At this point, I feel like pushing him off the roof myself.
ANDREA	I understand—
STELLA	What do you understand?
ANDREA	That you're fed up.
STELLA	And why do you think I'm fed up?
ANDREA	Well, the roof, the kite, the…
STELLA	Watch what you say. One more lie and I'll throw up.
ANDREA	You want the truth? He's fed up, too.
STELLA	With what?
ANDREA	With telling a mandarine from a nectarine, a nectarine from a tangerine, the whole routine.
STELLA	As in Greek cuisine.
ANDREA	It's not the same thing.
STELLA	Ha! You deserved expatriation. Justice does exist.
ANDREA	I don't understand.

STELLA	Look what you Greek men do to earn a living. In Greece, you would've died before you went to the market or washed a dish.
ANDREA	You're right. You both need a change.
STELLA	What do you suggest? Maybe I should come up and vent my frustrations on the roof, too?
ANDREA	Stella!
STELLA	Of course, I'm a woman.
ANDREA	At least he doesn't have cancer. And as long as you're healthy—
STELLA	I know, you have to count your blessings.
ANDREA	Don't knock it.
STELLA	Ah, *panayitsa mou*! What's wrong with me? Forgive me, Andrea. How is Marika? With all his craziness... How is your wife?
ANDREA	Better. She's not ready to move mountains yet, but she's better.
STELLA	Thank heavens. And your daughter?
ANDREA	She's finally decided to leave her husband.
STELLA	Is she taking the kids?
ANDREA	Of course.
STELLA	Good for her! It takes courage.
ANDREA	Sometimes I wonder if I'm being punished for forcing her to marry a Greek.
STELLA	Why? Do you really think her pretty blond boyfriend would have put her on a pedestal?
ANDREA	I know, there are Canadian men who beat their wives too.

STELLA   At least this way, you don't need an interpreter to
          talk to your grandchildren.

          *GEORGE appears on the roof and says to
          DIMITRI.*

GEORGE   Are you going to stop banging on the roof? We can't
          hear ourselves think downstairs!

DIMITRI   How come you're still at her place anyway? You
          showing her how you play with your paintbrush?

GEORGE   I don't play with my paintbrushes! Aren't you ever
          going to get that into your heads? I work with them!
          My work is just as honest and necessary as yours!

ANDREA   Stop talking nonsense, and tell him what she said.

GEORGE   It's all settled.

STELLA   *(amazed)* She's going to move?

GEORGE   There's no need…

DIMITRI   I knew it!

ANDREA   Let him finish.

DIMITRI   She wrapped him round her little finger!

GEORGE   That's right, the minute she saw me, she opened her
          legs and shouted: "Open House."

DIMITRI   I wouldn't be surprised, they're all the same.

GEORGE   Even your wife?

STELLA   What!

DIMITRI   *(about to slap him)* Don't you dare talk about your
          mother like that!

ANDREA   Mitso, he was joking… *(to GEORGE)* He was talking
          about *Québécois* women, idiot.

GEORGE   Of course, he knows them so well…

DIMITRI   Yes, *Monsieur*, I see hundreds of them every day, with their tight pants and their empty pockets.

GEORGE   If you took the time to talk to your tenant, instead of playing King Kong on the roof, you'd see she's not the kind of girl you think she is.

DIMITRI   I knew it! He sold his soul to her!

GEORGE   Honest to God!

DIMITRI   At least your uncle thinks of what's best for his family first.

ANDREA   Don't mix me up in this. *(to STELLA)* He doesn't know what he's saying anymore.

DIMITRI   *(He continues talking to GEORGE.)* Just wait till you show up at my store next time... I'll give all those vegetables you bum off me to Turkish refugees! Yes, I'd rather give it them to the Turks! At least they have some sense of family solidarity!

          Suddenly we hear the voice of a young woman.

CÉLINE   *(voice off) Monsieur* Dimitri!

          DIMITRI freezes and CÉLINE appears. GEORGE speaks to her in Québécois with only the slightest trace of an accent.

GEORGE   *Je vais lui expliquer.* Let me do the talking

CÉLINE   *J'suis capable de me défendre.*

GEORGE   *Il comprend pas bien le français.*

CÉLINE   *C'est son problème.*

ANDREA   *(to GEORGE) Qu'est-ce que toi racontes? (to CÉLINE) Bonzour, moi André frère de* Dzimmy. *(to GEORGE) Toi* crazy? *Ton papa* have big store and no speak *français*? Is that logical, *madame*? Dzimmy speak excellent *français*.

STELLA   Especially when he's yelling at me.

CÉLINE   *Bonjour, Madame Stella. Ça va? Vous avez l'air fatiguée.*

STELLA   I—

ANDREA   *(to GEORGE)* Could you go call the restaurant and tell them I've been delayed?

STELLA   *(Fanning herself with one hand.)* Verrry hot.

GEORGE   I have a call to make myself...

CÉLINE   *Chaud. Il fait chaud.*

GEORGE   ...But I'm afraid he'll throw her off the roof.

STELLA   *Oui, beaucoup saud. Beaucoup ormones.*

CÉLINE   Hormones?

         ANDREA, who overheard this last comment, pulls CÉLINE away, saying to GEORGE.

ANDREA   *Pourquoi* you not explain to *madame? Toi* forget *grec pour* translate? *(to CÉLINE)* Dzimmy say sorry *pour* noise. *(stamps his foot)* Bang, bang.

DIMITRI   I never said that! *(to CÉLINE)* No! *Moi,* no sorry *pour* noise!

GEORGE   See what I mean?

DIMITRI   *(to ANDREA)* So get the hell out of here! I don't need an interpreter!

STELLA   Somebody give him a cigarette. Can't you see he needs a fix?

CÉLINE   *(to DIMITRI)* Hey! *Je peux-tu parler là?*

ANDREA   Sure, sure. Dzimmy *parler touzours de toi.* "Nice girl!" he say.

DIMITRI   *(between clenched teeth)* Andrea!

CÉLINE   *Monsieur Dimitri, j'sais, c'est moi qui devrais m'excuser.* I come here to say I'm sorry *pour la musique.*

STELLA	*Pour la mouzique?* *(to GEORGE)* What did you tell her? That it's her music that's keeping your poor *papa* awake at night?
CÉLINE	*(to GEORGE) Qu'est-ce qu'elle dit?*
ANDREA	Stella say *mouzique zolie, romantique.*
CÉLINE	*Ouais, romantique* like a hangover.
ANDREA	Yes, like Nana Mouskouri.
CÉLINE	*(to GEORGE) Tu m'as pas dit que c'était à cause de la musique?*
ANDREA	Like Zorze Moustaki. You know Zorze Moustaki?
CÉLINE	*Qui?* Who?
GEORGE	A French singer born in Greece.
CÉLINE	Oh.
ANDREA	*Oui, Grecs* like *mouzique français.*
DIMITRI	Have you finished babbling?
CÉLINE	*(indicating DIMITRI) Pas lui en tout cas.*
ANDREA	Not true. Dzimmy like Zorze Guétary.
CÉLINE & **GEORGE**	Who!? *Qui!?*

ANDREA pushes his nephew towards the exit.

ANDREA	Let me deal with this. Go call my restaurant.
GEORGE	*(to CÉLINE) Je reviens dans deux minutes.* My uncle will explain everything to you. I have to make a phone call.

ANDREA picks up a plate of baklava while STELLA speaks to DIMITRI.

STELLA	She apologized…

DIMITRI I could care less about her apologies.

CÉLINE *(to ANDREA) Qu'est-ce qu'il dit?*

STELLA *(to DIMITRI, under her breath)* You'd rather have her strip for you?

ANDREA *(to CÉLINE)* Dzimmy like *beaucoup mouzique français,* but soft...

DIMITRI *(to STELLA)* Why did you say that?

ANDREA Dzimmy soft man... *toi comprends?*

STELLA *(to DIMITRI)* So you can give her a good spanking, the little sexpot.

ANDREA *(over his shoulder to STELLA)* It's not the sex that bothers him. She keeps him awake at night.

STELLA How come it doesn't bother me? It must be because my husband keeps me so happy in bed. *(DIMITRI gives her a murderous look.)* Oh! I beg your pardon, master. I'm getting a bit cynical in my old age too. Excuse me, *effendi.*

    STELLA goes off to drink her coffee in peace.

CÉLINE *Avez-vous fini là?* I can talk now?

ANDREA Sure, sweetheart. But first *toi* try this. *(He hands her the plate of baklava.) Pas dire* no. *Touzours* try first. *La vie est* full *de bonnes surprises.* Try. *C'est* Dzimmy he brought it *pour toi.*

DIMITRI Lay off, Andrea!

ANDREA *(to DIMITRI)* Okay, you tell her yourself. *(to CÉLINE) C'est ce que ze dis touzours:* This is Montreal. We talk, and make love, not war. *Manze, manze.*

CÉLINE *Parler de quoi?* Nothing to talk. He don't like music loud—*seulement bouzouki.*

ANDREA	No, *pas vrai*. Tenants before *grecs*. Dzimmy *dit*: "Bouzouki, no bouzouki, out, *mon hosti!*" Isn't that true, Stella?
STELLA	What?
ANDREA	She can't believe you're the one who makes such good baklava.
STELLA	Yes, I'm the one.
ANDREA	*(to CÉLINE)* You see? Stella too want them out.
STELLA	I wonder why I do it.
ANDREA	You know why Dzimmy kicked them out? Dzimmy give apartment for one person. *Après* two years, *avec cousins, cousines*, it was ten persons.
CÉLINE	*Une minute là!*
ANDREA	Sure, take your time. *Manze*.
CÉLINE	*Minute!* George he say it is my *musique*. Now I can't have visitors. It's my *appartement, non?*
ANDREA	Absolutely.
CÉLINE	*Alors que c'est qu'il veut?*
ANDREA	He tell you. Eh, Dzimmy?
STELLA	*(to herself)* I wonder why I go on doing it… *(She turns her empty demi-tasse upside-down on her saucer.)*
CÉLINE	*Qu'est-ce qu'elle a dit?*
STELLA	*(talking about "reading" her coffee grounds) Voir si moi* get money.
CÉLINE	*Ils veulent plus d'argent?* More money?
STELLA	*(to herself)* The rest will have to wait till another lifetime.
ANDREA	Dzimmy? Dzimmy does not give sit about money.

CÉLINE   Good, *parce qu'il n'aura pas un sou de plus.* Not one dollar more.

ANDREA   *Bravo! Z'aime femmes fortes.* Dzimmy likes strong women too. *Loui* like you so much *loui capable* give apartment to you *gratouitement.*

DIMITRI   Free apartment? What the hell is he talking about?

ANDREA   You see? Loui not even want mention *arzent. Pour ça* after thirty years he only have one store. *Même moi* I tell him: "Dzimmy, Dzimmy, *toi* too dzenerous. *Pourquoi* you give *frouta à madames gratouitement?*" *C'est* stupid, no?

CÉLINE   *Oui, mais moi je paie là* and I have right for all visit I want. I know the law. This is my country, *vous savez.* And if you people would care about our laws, not just to fill your pocket you would know I have the right for a *orchestre symphonique* in my *appartement* until eleven o'clock at night, every night and until tree in the morning, two times in a year. *(She takes a bite of her baklava, defiantly. STELLA turns to look at CÉLINE when she hears her raise her voice.)*

ANDREA   *(whispering to DIMITRI)* Now I understand how you feel. Suddenly I'd love to be that baklava!

DIMITRI   Pig!

ANDREA   You're right.

CÉLINE   *Quoi?*

ANDREA   *(to CÉLINE) Moi* explain *à Dzimmy ce que toi parle. (to DIMITRI)* She says we just came here for the money. Call her a racist and she'll do anything to prove she isn't.

STELLA   Ask her if she wants the baklava recipe. "Dzimmy" would be happy to go upstairs for dessert.

         DIMITRI glances at her, no longer knowing how to interpret her comments. STELLA gives him a little smile, then picks up her cup to "read" the grounds.

CÉLINE   *Qu'est-ce qu'elle a dit là?*

ANDREA   *Elle demande* is your friend just visitor.

CÉLINE   *Mais c'est pas de vos affaires!*

ANDREA   *Madame,* when my brother *malade,* sick *parce que saque nouit loui penser à toi,* that's my business!

CÉLINE   *Quoi? Il pense à moi?* He thinks of me in night?

DIMITRI   I'm leaving. *(He walks away.)*

ANDREA   *Oui,* your room over his bed. *Saque nouit:* creak-creak, creak-creak noise. *Tou comprends?*

CÉLINE   *Du bruit.*

ANDREA   *Oui...*

STELLA   *(to DIMITRI who has bent over to pick up his kite)* Is it supposed to rain tonight?

ANDREA   ...Dzimmy like to do creak-creak *aussi. Saque nuit. Dzénérousment.* But *sans* noise.

DIMITRI   *(looking at STELLA)* No. Why?

ANDREA   *Toi?* Understand?

STELLA   *(answering DIMITRI)* You'll see.

ANDREA   *Quand* Dzimmy make creak-creak, nobody know. *Zouste* him and woman. *Tou comprends ce que ze dis?*

CÉLINE   *(furious)* Oh! *Le vieux snoro!*

ANDREA   *Qui?* Dzimmy?

CÉLINE   *J'aurais dû le deviner. Crac-crac. Toute la nuit. (She turns to DIMITRI who's watching STELLA put her cup back on the tray and pick up the others.) Monsieur Dimitri!*

ANDREA   Wait! *Toi pas compris mon français. Moi* explain in English.

STELLA   What's going on?

ANDREA	She wants to take him to court!
CÉLINE	*Monsieur Dimitri…*

> *She takes his arm gently. DIMITRI freezes.*
> *ANDREA is reassured by her change of attitude*
> *says.*

ANDREA	Dzimmy. *Zouste Dzimmy.*
CÉLINE	I like better Dimitri.
ANDREA	Did you hear that? Smile, you idiot!
CÉLINE	*Monsieur* Dimitri, why you not tell me my father don't let you sleep?
ANDREA	Your father?
CÉLINE	He cannot sleep on sofa, because he has back pain, so I give him my bed. But I did not know he make noise at night also.
ANDREA	*(hand to forehead)* Stupid me! *(to STELLA)* I misunderstood. *(to CÉLINE) Dimitri avait raison. (to STELLA)* It's her father who works at the court. *(to CÉLINE)* Dimitri said, *monsieur* too old *pour être* son boyfriend.
CÉLINE	He not so old.
ANDREA	Dimitri just say old compared to you, so young, so smart, so *zolie…*
CÉLINE	*J'suis déjà sortie avec un gars plus vieux que lui.*
ANDREA	Oh. *(to DIMITRI)* You hear that? She went out with a guy who was older than you.
DIMITRI	Slime!
ANDREA	*(to CÉLINE) C'est vrai.* He says, in life, you must try everything. All ages, all *nationalités.*
DIMITRI	Pimp!

ANDREA   *(to DIMITRI)* You're right. I should mind my own
         business. Your turn to play.

CÉLINE   *Il est encore fâché?*

ANDREA   *Loui va expliquer.*

CÉLINE   *Expliquer quoi?*

ANDREA   I have to go back to work.

CÉLINE   I have nothing to explain! He is my father, and he
         can stay as long as he want!

ANDREA   Bravo! Bravo! Dimitri was right. *Toi excellente*
         daughter. Bravo! It make my heart smile, a girl who
         love her father like that! *(He forces his pack of cigarettes
         into DIMITRI's hand.)* You're going to need them. I'll
         take care of Stella.

DIMITRI Andrea!

ANDREA   Stella, sweetheart, I'm going to have to bother you.
         But it's your own fault.

STELLA   *(as she finishes gathering up the cups)* Now what have
         I done?

ANDREA   Your baklava. She ate mine and made it look so
         good, I've got a real craving.

CÉLINE   *(to DIMITRI who looks lost)* Qu'est-ce que vous voulez
         m'expliquer?

ANDREA   Just two little pieces. If you don't mind going
         downstairs for them…

STELLA   I was on my way down anyway.

ANDREA   God bless your pretty hands. *(He kisses her hands.)*
         Ever since my Marika's been sick, I've had to eat the
         baklava we serve our customers.

CÉLINE   Hey! Explain what? I don't have all day.

ANDREA   *(to CÉLINE) Ton papa* like souvlaki? *(He takes one of
         her hands in his.)* Come to my restaurant *avec ton papa*

and eat all you want. On the house. *(He kisses her hand.)*

CÉLINE   *Eh ben!* You are a real gentleman, *merci.*

ANDREA   *Nous* Greek men, all like that. That is why, *beaucoup de* lady tourists in Greece. *(to DIMITRI)* Remember the Gordian knot. Slash! *(to STELLA)* You have to spell it out with Dzimmy. Otherwise she'll walk all over him.

STELLA   *(sarcastically)* Poor guy.

ANDREA   He's too soft-hearted.

STELLA   Right.

ANDREA   Too soft-hearted.

STELLA   Here, you take the tray. *(She passes it to ANDREA.)* If it's not asking too much of a soft-hearted guy like you.

ANDREA   *Avec plaisir, madame. Au revoir, mademoiselle.*

CÉLINE   Céline.

ANDREA   Céline. *Comme c'est beau!*

STELLA   *(to DIMITRI)* Try to get it over with fast. I'm going to need the roof.

> *She turns towards the exit where, covering her eyes so as not to see the drop, she waits for ANDREA who says to CÉLINE.*

ANDREA   Ah! If I more young like Dimitri, *ze te ploumerais!* *(He turns towards the exit singing.)* Alouette, *zentille alouette!* Alouette, don't forget my restaurant! *Tou peux manzer* ten lobsters! *Tou peux manzer* ten *salades.* Ten souvlakis! Twenty baklavas! *Gratouit! Café compris! Zouste* bring your own wine!

> *He exits, followed by STELLA who tries not to look down. DIMITRI stares helplessly at the pack of cigarettes.*

CÉLINE   He very funny your brother. *(to herself) Dommage que toute la famille soit pas comme lui. (DIMITRI opens the pack of cigarettes.)* You start smoking again? *(DIMITRI looks at her surprised.)* Your son, he said you are grouchy because you stop smoking.

DIMITRI   *Oui, arrêter…* Every day, for one month, I try new kind. Last week I say: "What you looking for? They all the same. *Tout la même soze.*" *(He studies the pack.)*

CÉLINE   So now, you start again because of my father.

DIMITRI   No… *(He slips the pack back into his pocket.)*

CÉLINE   *Je m'excuse.*

DIMITRI   …Not your papa.

CÉLINE   At home in Saguenay, he has big open space, so here *en appartement* in Montreal—

DIMITRI   I say not your papa!

CÉLINE   Hey! Don't yell! I'm not Greek!

DIMITRI   So, listen to me! I say not *ton papa. C'est le noise* since one month.

CÉLINE   *Moi, je fais du bruit?*

DIMITRI   *Oui! Comme ça…* *(He takes a few steps.)*

CÉLINE   *Ben oui. (walking)*

DIMITRI   *Moi* cannot wats news because *toi fais…* *(two or three heavy steps)* over my television. *Moi* cannot eat because *toi fais…* *(two or three small steps)* over my table!

CÉLINE   *Excusez-moi*, I cannot fly!

DIMITRI   Alone, *touzours* alone…

CÉLINE   So? Is that a problem?

DIMITRI   *Oui!*

CÉLINE	*Pardon?*
DIMITRI	*Oui,* it's a problem. If *beaucoup...* *(He hops up and and down.)*
CÉLINE	*Beaucoup de pas.*
DIMITRI	Tsildren, *bébés, grand-mamá,* no bother me...
CÉLINE	No bother you?!
DIMITRI	...But alone *touzours, seule.* I think: Why always alone? She's sick? In my store, I wats girls like you, they buy one avocado, one *tomate,* one, one, never two. *Pourquoi?,* I ask. Only sick persons in hospital *touzours* alone *comme ça...*
CÉLINE	I'm not always alone.
DIMITRI	You have fiancé?
CÉLINE	*Ecoutez,* I don't want talk to you about my *problèmes.*
DIMITRI	You have *problème?*
CÉLINE	Non—*pourquoi j'ai dit ça*—I have no *problèmes.* Not really.
DIMITRI	That's what I say to myself. *Quel problème?* You young, you *parle français,* no war, *beaucoup* bread, *beaucoup* freedom, *beaucoup* education, good work... Why you laughing at me?
CÉLINE	I don't laugh. I smile.
DIMITRI	*Pourquoi?* You think I say *stupide* things?
CÉLINE	*Ben non.* I smile because you talk like my father. He says the same things to me for tree days.
DIMITRI	Because *ton papa* love you... he want you to be happy.
CÉLINE	*Mais je me sens très bien.* I am happy.
DIMITRI	Alone...

CÉLINE	*Il y a autre chose dans la vie, vous savez.* There's more in life than just marriage and children...
DIMITRI	*Quoi?*
CÉLINE	*Ecoutez—*
DIMITRI	*Oui?* What is there besides *la familia?*
CÉLINE	I have to go now. I leave something on the stove.
DIMITRI	*S'il vous plaît,* I want to know.
CÉLINE	But why do you care?
DIMITRI	You not want to know what I have here and here? *(indicates his heart and his head)*
CÉLINE	*Pas en ce moment.* Some other time.
DIMITRI	*Pourquoi?* Because I am stupid immigrant?
CÉLINE	Whoa! No *paranoia raciste,* okay?
DIMITRI	*Moi aussi* I have something here and here, not just *familia* and work, *vous savez...*
CÉLINE	*Oui.* I am sure.
DIMITRI	*Alors pourquoi* you never speak to me? You here one month. Every day you talk to your *satte.*
CÉLINE	*A qui?* Who?
DIMITRI	*Ton satte*—miaow-miaow.
CÉLINE	Ah, *mon chat. Chat.*
DIMITRI	*Toi parler avec satte* every day. I hear. "Minou, minou, minou!" One hour. Two hours! "Minou, minou, minou!" *Et moi?* You speak with me one minute? No! You think I can't understand everything you say. But how can I learn to understand you if you never speak to me, *zamais?* I have other things to say, not just *(with a Québécois accent)* "*Patates* New Brunswick *cette semaine, cinq* kilos *pour oune piasse!*" *Oui,* I have *beaucoup* things I want to say to him, to her, to you,

but I don't have words. Because no one ever talk to me about anything except price of *patates*. So everyone think all Dimitri knows how to talk about is *patates*. And there are days when Dimitri think all he got here and here, *c'est patates*!

CÉLINE   *Eh ben…. Je m'excuse…. Vraiment….* It's not because I don't want to talk to you. *Vous savez….* Me, I don't know what I am looking for also. Like you with your kinds of cigarettes. But I am fine, really. I'm happy with my cat. I know, you think, "A woman, she's not made to talk, to sleep with a cat!" But when I wake up, I still feel like a woman. Before, with my boyfriend, I was only a woman when he was lying on me. But why am I telling you this. *(beat)* Sometimes I don't understand myself. It's not a question of language. *Alors parlons d'autre chose. Vous voulez? Monsieur Dimitri? (She touches his lips.)* Show me you're not mad at me any more. *Faites-moi un sourire.*

> DIMITRI *has frozen at her touch.*

Un sourire. You know what that mean? No, to look at you, I think there is no word for it in Greek. *Hamoyélo?* Your son taught me. George says it doesn't make us so tired to smile. It takes just fourteen muscles. And to make the baboon face, it takes seventy-two. *Alors faites comme il dit:* smile, save energy.

DIMITRI   *Ze comprends pas.*

CÉLINE   *Les patates du Nouveau-Brunswick…* is it true, five kilos of potatoes for one dollar?

DIMITRI   *Oui.* Big special this week.

CÉLINE   Yesterday at Metro, I paid one ninety-nine!

DIMITRI   *(revived) Pourquoi* you do that? Like my tsildren! You find dollars in the street?

CÉLINE   *(laughing)* You talk like my father again!

DIMITRI   One ninety-nine!

CÉLINE   Okay, *j'ai compris*. From now on, I come to your store. Every day. Are you happy?

DIMITRI   *(looking at her)* I say that for you. *Pour toi* to save money.

CÉLINE   Don't worry. I am very careful to my money. Because I want to make many *voyages*.

DIMITRI   So why you don't get smaller *appartement?* A little smaller less expensive?

CÉLINE   *(laughing)* You really want me to leave! *Que c'est que je vous ai fait? (DIMITRI stares at her.) Pourquoi vous me répondez pas?* What did I do? *(Suddenly there's a gust of wind that lifts the kite ever so slightly.)* Ah! He is beautiful. Is he yours?

DIMITRI   *Ben non. Moi* too old *pour ça.*

CÉLINE   You're not so old.

DIMITRI   It must be the light. Like they use on the old tsicken at Provigo.

CÉLINE   Make him fly.

DIMITRI   Then everyone say Dimitri become *bébé!*

CÉLINE   *Je trouve pas ça bébé, moi.*

DIMITRI   No?

CÉLINE   Ben non. *(She passes the kite to him.)* Make him fly. I've never held a *cerf-volant*… a kite. *S'il vous plaît.*

DIMITRI   Okay, okay! *Ze faire voler. (He gently pushes her away and checks to see whether anyone is looking.) Ze faire voler. (He wets his index finger and holds it in the air, muttering to himself.)* What did I get myself into now! *Ti malakas!*

CÉLINE   Hey! *Si vous voulez qu'on parle,* no Greek!

DIMITRI   Ze dis not enough wind…

CÉLINE	He won't fly.
DIMITRI	*Meilleur temps, c'est printemps.* Wind always warm and strong in spring. You just let go and it go high, high like bird. You can fly a kite in late summer, but it take longer... *beaucoup* work, *beaucoup* patience...
CÉLINE	I am not *pressée. (DIMITRI glances at her again.)* It must be beautiful to watch him fly, eh? Like a big bird.
DIMITRI	*Oui, c'est....* Like when you dance...?
CÉLINE	*Quand je danse, moi?*
DIMITRI	Alone.
CÉLINE	How do you know *je* danse alone sometimes?
DIMITRI	*Beaucoup danses grecques* for men alone. *Tou sais?* Like Turkiss derviss dance when he pray. *Comme ça... (He spins around two or three times.)* He turn, he turn, *plous vite, plous vite, comme ça...* and while he turn, his soul rise, higher and higher and fly free like a bird.... *Comme ça avec...*
CÉLINE	*Le cerf-volant.*
DIMITRI	*Le cerf-volant.*
CÉLINE	*C'est ça.*
DIMITRI	*Aétos.*
CÉLINE	*Aétos...*
DIMITRI	It also mean eagle. *Toi* know bird eagle?
CÉLINE	*L'aigle.*
DIMITRI	*Oui.* In Greek, *cerf-volant* and eagle are same word.
CÉLINE	*Aétos.*
DIMITRI	*C'est ça.* A paper eagle. *(He smiles at last.) Ouais...* When I was little, it was only way to leave my village, to fly like eagle, far away from planes and

bombs and houses burned to ground, fly away until you reats other beautiful houses, other countries...

CÉLINE   *Le cerf-volant,* he made you dream.

DIMITRI   *Ah! Oui.* It made me dream.

CÉLINE   *Comme l'aurore boréale.*

DIMITRI   Eh?

CÉLINE   *Comment on dit ça en anglais.... Aurora borealis?* Maybe it's from Greek.

DIMITRI   *Borealis?*

CÉLINE   At home in Saguenay, my boyfriend and me, we watched it and imagined we could ride it to the other side of the Pole, and land in hot countries where every noise and smell would be new. *(Dimitri is too busy trying to launch the kite to listen to her.)* "On va finir par revenir" he said. If we always come back, why leave? Idiot! Now he think he can send my father to play me some love songs, and I'll swim back up the river like a *saumon....* But you, when you were a big boy, you did not change your idea, you followed your kite.... Is it expensive to live in Greece?

DIMITRI   I don't know. It's been a long time.

CÉLINE   *Oui...* you, you are happy here.

DIMITRI   *Ouais,* so so.

CÉLINE   *Comment ça,* so so? You're not happy to be in Québec?

DIMITRI   *Très* happy. Back in Greece, when I saw our house burn, I say to myself: "I only want one thing in life, one thing: to have a house in a country where no one can burn it down. A house where I can grow old and die in peace.... *C'est tout.* Now I have house, I have quiet, I have good wife...

CÉLINE   So, what more do you want? *(He turns to look at her. Suddenly the kite rises.)* Wow! Can I hold him?

DIMITRI   Sure. *Mais attention. Comme ça.*

            CÉLINE holds the string with him.

CÉLINE   *Regardez-moi ça!* Look how high! Frrr! *C'est vrai...* I feel like I'm flying with him. Like a magic carpet!

            STELLA reappears, followed by GEORGE. She is carrying two blankets and a pillow.

GEORGE   You can't do this!

STELLA   Why not? Because I'm a woman? Or because I'm a Greek woman? *(She looks at DIMITRI and CÉLINE.)* Ah, looks like the summit conference was a success. You even got your gust of wind.

CÉLINE   You so lucky, *Madame* Stella, you have husband *très romantique* like *Monsieur* Dimitri.

            STELLA looks at DIMITRI who has frozen in his tracks.

STELLA   *Oui, beaucoup* lucky. *(to herself, "in Greek," as she spreads out her blankets next to the bottle of Retsina)* Sure. Every morning I thank the Virgin Mary, because every night my Dimitraki takes me for a kite ride.

            GEORGE goes over to DIMITRI at the front end of the roof.

GEORGE   Great! Bravo!

DIMITRI   Now what have I done?

GEORGE   She intends to spend the night on the roof. *(DIMITRI looks at him.)* Did you hear me? She wants to spend the night on the roof. *(DIMITRI looks at STELLA.)* Go talk to her, *Babá.* I'll help Céline hold the kite. *(He takes the string.)* Pis, c'est le fun, le cerf-volant?

CÉLINE   Oh, *oui! (whispering)* Qu'est-ce qui se passe?

GEORGE	My mother wants to spend the night on the roof with my father.
CÉLINE	Oh! *C'est beau*, at their age!!
GEORGE	They've always been that way. *J'ai une surprise pour toi.*

> *GEORGE whispers something in her ear. DIMITRI walks up to STELLA apprehensively.*

DIMITRI	Why?
STELLA	We'll discuss it tomorrow.
DIMITRI	Stella…
STELLA	I said tomorrow!
DIMITRI	Just because I came up on the roof?
STELLA	Dimitri, either you all leave me alone, or I'll go spend the night in the park!

> *She arranges her pillow. DIMITRI stares at her, taken aback by her determined tone of voice.*

CÉLINE	*(to GEORGE) T'es pas sérieux!*
GEORGE	*Mais oui.* When you told me how much you wanted to see their show…
CÉLINE	*(whispering)* How did you do it? The show was sold out the first day.

> *GEORGE whispers in her ear again. STELLA has sat down. DIMITRI hasn't budged.*

STELLA	What's the matter? You can't get along without your servant for one night?
DIMITRI	I treat you like a servant?
STELLA	It's true, you never had to order me to do anything. I was so well trained, I can tell when a man is thirsty by the way he smacks his lips.

DIMITRI   And me, I give nothing...

STELLA   Oh, you've given a lot. And in return for what you've given, you probably expected me to wash your feet when you got home from work, the way your mother washed your father's...

DIMITRI   Are you serious?

STELLA   Stay calm, Stella. You swore you'd stay calm. Calm. *(She empties her glass of wine.)*

CÉLINE   *Ah, j'suis tout excitée!*

GEORGE   *Moi aussi, tu sais pas comment!* Last night—I'm not kidding—last night, I was so depressed, I was down on my hands and knees talking to a spider.

CÉLINE   *(laughing) Que c'est que tu lui disais?*

> *GEORGE murmurs something in her ear, while, at the other end of the roof, STELLA uncorks her bottle.*

DIMITRI   Don't tell me you're going to start drinking too...

> *STELLA turns on the music, fills her glass and starts to drink.*

CÉLINE   ...if us humans exist?

GEORGE   Whenever I run out of inspiration, I see death everywhere. In every speck of dust I breathe, in every fruit I eat, in every drop of water I drink. Somewhere in all that, I think, there must be a microscopic trace of an old warrior who died of boredom a hundred years ago, of a little girl lost in a snowstorm a thousand years ago, of a dinosaur...

DIMITRI   *(He can't stand to see her drink.)* Stella, stop!

> *He leans over to take the glass away from her.*

STELLA   Or what? *(She turns off the music.)* Or what? Will you try to evict me too, if I don't fulfill all your desires!

> *Alerted by her shouting, GEORGE and CÉLINE turn to look at STELLA.*

DIMITRI (*shaken*) Why did you say that?

STELLA Just a warning. (*She drinks her wine.*)

CÉLINE *Qu'est-ce qui se passe?*

GEORGE I never should have told her how much the tickets cost. Now she's accusing my father of setting a bad example for me with his largess...

CÉLINE I was going to pay for mine. How much were they? Thirty, thirty-five dollars?

GEORGE A hundred.

CÉLINE *Hein!*

GEORGE After I spent an hour bargaining with a scalper on the phone.

> *DIMITRI goes over to GEORGE.*

DIMITRI Were you there when your uncle went downstairs with her?

GEORGE Yes.

DIMITRI What did he say to her?

GEORGE *Thio* Andrea?

DIMITRI Yes. What did he tell your mother?

GEORGE Nothing. He took his baklava and left.

DIMITRI That's all?

GEORGE Yeah.

DIMITRI So why is she pulling this Lysistrata act on me?

> *GEORGE shrugs, more interested in what CÉLINE has to say.*

CÉLINE *Cent dollars...*

GEORGE	It's worth a thousand.
CÉLINE	I like them, but...
GEORGE	I'm not talking about the group. I'm talking about... *Ah, j'sais pas comment le dire.* It's not just because I'm shy, I'm no good with words. And I'm afraid you'll say no...

STELLA gargles with her wine.

CÉLINE	No? *Pourquoi?*
GEORGE	An hour ago, I felt.... I felt like this kite.... Just hanging on to life by a string. It felt like I was lost in the night, then suddenly.... This might sound corny, but when I saw you, it was like the sun was finally rising. Suddenly I saw enough shapes and colours to fill a thousand paintings—if you accept to pose for me. So please, don't talk about money. I would have bought the tickets, even if they cost two hundred dollars.
DIMITRI	*(to STELLA)* You know what? You don't deserve me.
STELLA	So you finally admit it.
DIMITRI	Yes. You deserved someone like Andrea. He would've put you through the paces. Because Andrea figured you women out ages ago.
STELLA	What did Andrea the Great figure out?
DIMITRI	Just wait and see. Thank God, I've still got a few good years left.

He turns away and nervously takes out the pack of cigarettes. Meanwhile.

CÉLINE	*C'est fou.* People in Montreal are so nice. People aren't so friendly in Québec City. When I was working there and I said I came from Saguenay, they called me a *"bleuet"* and told me to go home.
GEORGE	*Hein?*

CÉLINE	They thought we come to steal their jobs.
GEORGE	*C'est si beau, la ville de Québec...*
CÉLINE	*Oh, la ville est magnifique.* But the people, they don't like outsiders, I was forced to spend all my time with other *"bleuets."*
GEORGE	Why didn't you go home?
CÉLINE	No work.
GEORGE	For a nurse? There are sick people everywhere.
CÉLINE	I was tired working with genetic sickness. My region, it's been closed off from the rest of the province for three hundred years.

> *STELLA turns to DIMITRI who is staring at the pack of cigarettes.*

STELLA	I'm waiting.
DIMITRI	You can stop waiting. I'm leaving and I won't be coming home tonight.
STELLA	Have fun.
DIMITRI	Maybe I won't come home tomorrow either.
STELLA	Good riddance.
DIMITRI	If that's the way you feel...
STELLA	Did you expect me to throw myself at your feet?

> *STELLA lies down. DIMITRI stares at her while GEORGE looks at CÉLINE and says.*

GEORGE	*Un bleuet. Un bleuet blond.* A pretty blond blueberry.... Fate works in strange ways! I can hardly wait to tell you about all the images I see, the colours, the poses.... Why don't we have a bite to eat before the show—oops!

> *The kite begins to tug at the string. The wind is rising and the sun is beginning to set. While*

> GEORGE *and* CÉLINE *laugh and try to control the kite*, DIMITRI, *who is still staring at his wife, says.*

DIMITRI   What a fool I was, wanting to spend the rest of my life with you…

STELLA   Because I know where your socks are, how you like your coffee, what days you take your bath…

DIMITRI   If you think that's the only reason…

STELLA   So you admit that it's one reason? *(She has sat up again.)*

DIMITRI   Talking to you is impossible.

STELLA   Sure. I'm not as intelligent and understanding as—

DIMITRI   As who?

STELLA   As your spiders.

DIMITRI   You see what I mean? You turn everything I say into a joke. It's obvious, you can't stand me anymore.

STELLA   I just finished bringing up two kids. You think I want to spend the rest of my life nursing a frustrated grocer?

DIMITRI   Okay, I get the point.

STELLA   What point, genius?

DIMITRI   I've never been anything but a grocer for you.

STELLA   And what have I been for you?

DIMITRI   *(turning away from her)* Just wait and see. There are lots of people who can still appreciate me for what I'm worth.

STELLA   *(She stands up, but* DIMITRI *has already walked over to* CÉLINE.*)* WHAT HAVE I BEEN FOR YOU?

DIMITRI   *(to* CÉLINE*)* Don't forget. *Beaucoup* specials *auzourd'hui. Gourganes* from Saguenay too. One nineteen a pound.

CÉLINE	*D'accord. Je viendrai un peu plus tard.* See you later.
STELLA	*(to DIMITRI)* Don't forget your kite. If you fly it over your store the days of your big romantic specials, I'm sure you'll attract lots of pretty new customers.

> *She sits down again. DIMITRI turns towards her.*

GEORGE	Aren't we having supper together?
CÉLINE	I would like that, but I have my father. He don't like to eat alone.
GEORGE	Maybe we can have a drink after the show, unless you have to tuck him in, too?

> *DIMITRI and STELLA both turn toward their son.*

STELLA	So the tickets were for her?
GEORGE	What tickets?
STELLA	What tickets! *(She stands up.)* The tickets you managed to bargain down to fifty dollars a piece on the phone. You think I don't understand English either?
GEORGE	She's going to pay me back.
STELLA	Right, in pubic hair. With a few diseases as a bonus!
GEORGE	*(to DIMITRI)* Will you tell her to stop yelling!
STELLA	One hundred dollars!
CÉLINE	*(to GEORGE)* Is she still mad about the tickets?
STELLA	When I think of all the washrooms I cleaned for a hundred dollars!
GEORGE	*(to CÉLINE)* No, she thinks we're having supper in a restaurant.
STELLA	And all the lunches I ate in those washrooms to save two dollars!
GEORGE	Yell a bit louder. They can't hear you in Laval.

STELLA   I hope they do hear me. I've been killing myself for thirty years, so everything would look good, acting like your *caca* smelled sweet! Yours, your sister's, your father's. Let them hear the truth. *Monsieur* just spent two sleepless nights and he's up on the roof. Why should I tell the neighbours we were just taking a sunbath? I haven't been able to sleep more than two hours a night for years myself. Did anyone ever ask me why? *(DIMITRI lowers his eyes. STELLA glares at CÉLINE.)* A hundred dollars for that! I could understand it, from an old man...

GEORGE   At least she takes an interest in my work.

STELLA   *(sizing up CÉLINE)* Sure. She looks like the type who'd clean fifteen washrooms to buy you a paintbrush.

CÉLINE   *Qu'est-ce qu'elle a dit?*

STELLA   Ask her if she'd wash a single public toilet to buy you some paint.

GEORGE   *(to CÉLINE)* She wants to know if you like tripe soup.

CÉLINE   *(making a face) La soupe aux tripes?*

STELLA   I knew it! It's easy to talk about harmonious colours and dynamic shapes. But nobody would take me out for a cup of coffee, even at six in the morning. They're ashamed to be seen with me. *(She turns away, as if to hide her tears.)*

CÉLINE   *Pourquoi elle parle de la soupe aux tripes?*

GEORGE   She thinks I spend too much money in restaurants, so she wants us to have supper with them. Your father's invited too. *(to STELLA)* Me, I'm ashamed of you?

CÉLINE   *Madame Stella?*

STELLA   *(to DIMITRI)* Why don't you say anything? Did he ever take you out for a cup of coffee?

CÉLINE	*Madame Stella, c'est moi qui l'a invité.*
GEORGE	Did either one of you ever wonder why?
STELLA	Forget it, it's too painful.
CÉLINE	*C'est vrai.* I invited him to thank him.
STELLA	*(to DIMITRI)* Now what's she talking about?
GEORGE	Don't change the subject. How many times have I heard you tell me how much you both sacrificed so I could have a better life. As if you never did anything for your own pleasure. And when I try to talk about what I want to do with that life, you make fun of my dream. Do you think it's fun spending time with people who have nothing but reproaches for you? Why? Because my work doesn't earn enough to buy me a Cadillac that you can show off to the neighbours when I come to visit?
STELLA	It's not because you chose to be a painter, my boy. Some painters own two Cadillacs…
GEORGE	No! I won't start painting sad clowns or playful pussycats just to make you happy. And if you're ashamed of me, I won't come by anymore. Because I'll always ride a bike. And I hope my kids will too.
STELLA	Your kids?
GEORGE	The kids I'll have some day.
STELLA	*(looking at CÉLINE) Ah, panayitsa mou.*
CÉLINE	*(to GEORGE) Que c'est qu'il y a encore?*
STELLA	*(to GEORGE)* Do you have enough money left for a box of prophylactics?
GEORGE	Here we go! *(to DIMITRI)* Why did you let her drink? You know she can't handle it!

> *STELLA is, in fact, a bit tipsy, otherwise she would never dare admit the things she's going to say a bit later.*

STELLA	Now what did I say wrong! You know you're going to do it, so you may as well be prepared. *(to DIMITRI)* Give him some money.
GEORGE	I don't want any! *(to CÉLINE)* Oh my God! She still believes it's humiliating for a man to let a woman pay.
CÉLINE	*(cautiously)* I heard her say *prophylactiques*.
STELLA	Ah ha! That she understands.
GEORGE	*(to DIMITRI)* Here, hold the kite. Take the string before I strangle her with it!
CÉLINE	George, is she saying what I think?
STELLA	*Oui, oui.*
GEORGE	*Mamá!*
CÉLINE	*Pourquoi vous parlez de prophylactiques?*
GEORGE	She wants me to go buy a box for them so my father doesn't have to leave.
CÉLINE	*Hein? (to STELLA) Vous pouvez encore faire des bébés?*
STELLA	You better not, or I'll scratch your eyes out! *Diavole!*
CÉLINE	*Qu'est-ce qu'elle a dit?*
STELLA	Buy *beaucoup prophylactiques*. Because first night, five times.
GEORGE	*Mamá*, stop!
CÉLINE	First night?
STELLA	If he same as my husband…
CÉLINE	Yes?
STELLA	Five times.
CÉLINE	*Je comprends pas.*
GEORGE	She's bragging about Greek men.

STELLA   Sure, Greek men. Look at them stick out their chest, like father like son. All you have to do is stroke their balls…

CÉLINE   *Cinq fois?*

STELLA   First night. Yes. Big opening special. *(She reverts to speaking "Greek.")* Afterwards, you'll get as much attention as a vacuum cleaner. But it's not his fault. Why should he think that women have more feelings than a vacuum cleaner, when all his life he saw his mother act dumb just to make his father look good? Ach! You deserve what's happening to you, Stella. If your little prince has shoved you aside, you have only yourself to blame.

            She sits down beside her glass. DIMITRI has lowered his eyes. GEORGE is looking at his mother.

CÉLINE   It must have been beautiful…

GEORGE   What?

CÉLINE   Her wedding night. I didn't understand a thing, but I could hear the emotion in her voice.

GEORGE   Yes, I think we should leave them alone now. I'll be right back.

CÉLINE   *(to DIMITRI) Merci pour le cerf-volant. (He looks at her.)* Thank you for the *aétos. (She passes him the string.)* You have specials tomorrow also?

            DIMITRI nods. Meanwhile, GEORGE has gone to kneel beside his mother.

GEORGE   Would you pose for me, *Mademoiselle* Stella? I would like to paint your portrait. *(He takes his mother's hands to kiss them.)*

STELLA   To make your girlfriends laugh between two make-out sessions? Because if you were really serious, you would use a photograph from before I turned into a fossil!

GEORGE smiles.

GEORGE   Okay. *(He goes back to CÉLINE.)* She'll cook supper for us some other night. *(to DIMITRI)* Why don't you take her out for supper at a *café-terrasse?* There are bunches of them a block away.

DIMITRI   A block away.... You want my car too? Is that it? *(He is about to take out his keys.)*

GEORGE   No thanks. She has a car.

DIMITRI   Great! So now you don't need me either.

He turns his back to GEORGE who stares at him, more and more ill at ease.

GEORGE   Okay... *(to CÉLINE, choked up)* So, where are you taking me for supper?

CÉLINE   I'd like to try your uncle's restaurant.

She exits. GEORGE takes one last look at his parents and follows her. DIMITRI is looking at the kite, pensively. It's almost dark and the wind has risen.

STELLA   If he gets her pregnant, I swear, if my son gives me grandchildren who speak to me in French, I'm going to tie your damn kite around your neck and let the wind carry you away! *(beat)* Calm, Stella, calm. Have a drink. It will help you see the bright side of things. There's always a bright side. If your Yorgho falls in love with her, you'll get to see him more often. She lives right upstairs.... Ah, *panayitsa mou!* He'll be doing it right over my head. Now I won't be able to sleep at all! Why did you have to come up on the roof! Couldn't you have just gone knocking at her door? No, you had to get her up on the roof too! And how come you're still here? I thought you said you were going somewhere where people appreciate you for what you're really worth?

DIMITRI   I'm on my way. *(He tries to reel in the kite.)*

STELLA   Now that you've practised your French, I'm sure you'll attract them like flypaper.

> *She takes a drink of her wine. DIMITRI looks at her.*

DIMITRI   What are you trying to say?

STELLA   Forget it. It's the wine.

DIMITRI   Stella, she just wanted to explain why her father is so restless at night. What was I supposed to do? Block my ears?

> *He turns back to his kite. STELLA watches him, then says.*

STELLA   Why can't he sleep? *(DIMITRI doesn't answer.)* His wife has kicked him out? Is that why he's ended up at his daughter's house…. If he loves his wife, why doesn't he go tell her he loves her, instead of blasting us with his love songs! Eh? Unless he's glad his wife doesn't want anything to do with him…. That must be it. He's glad she wants nothing to do with him…

> *DIMITRI looks at STELLA. She lies down.*

DIMITRI   You have to be kidding. You're not going to spend the night on the roof—

STELLA   It's my roof too—

DIMITRI   But you're afraid of heights—

STELLA   In the dark, I won't realize where I am. *(She pulls the blanket over her.)* You can leave now. I'm anxious to ask the stars if at least they remember that I exist.

DIMITRI   Please, give me a break!

STELLA   I wasn't trying to be funny. When I was a girl, I used to tell the stars what I was going to do when I became a woman.

DIMITRI   You talked to the stars…

STELLA   Yes. Every time my mother's sobs prevented me from sleeping at night, I'd climb out of bed and go up on the roof to count the stars... *(She looks up at the stars.)* How many times, looking up at the stars, I swore I wouldn't end up like my mother, like her mother, like— *(She falls silent with a sob.)*

DIMITRI   Stella... *(She doesn't answer.)* Stella, if you insist upon sleeping outside tonight, I'll put a mattress out in the back yard—

STELLA   No. Too many walls, too many lights, too close to the kitchen.

DIMITRI   Forget the fucking kitchen!

STELLA   Don't tell me you're going to start yelling again!

DIMITRI   Every time I try to get close to you, you bring up the kitchen!

STELLA   Since when do you even notice I exist outside the kitchen?

DIMITRI   Here we go again!

He tugs at the kite. His only way of avoiding her questions, without losing face. STELLA stands up.

STELLA   Answer me. Have you ever come to me one single time, except when you wanted to fill your gut or empty your balls?

DIMITRI glares at her.

DIMITRI   I never should have let you drink!

STELLA   But it's very convenient, admit it. "Stella, you're drunk," then business as usual, back to the kitchen.

DIMITRI   Right.

STELLA watches him struggle with the kite.

STELLA   Sometimes, I swear, I think we'd have a lot more to say to each other if we didn't speak the same language. Sometimes, when I look at myself naked… *(DIMITRI stares at her.)* You didn't know that either, eh? That sometimes I stand naked in front of the big, beautiful mirror in our bedroom—

DIMITRI   *(tugging at the kite)* You better go downstairs and have a cup of strong coffee.

STELLA   Otherwise, you'll hit me? *(DIMITRI looks at her, sadly.)* It's true, you've never raised a hand to me. No, you slam the door. Like your father—

DIMITRI   Leave my father out of this!

STELLA   —and like my father. You slam the door, just like them. So I lock myself in the bedroom. And I stand naked in front of the mirror. It's not easy, believe me, with my mother's voice, my grandmother's voice, and the voices of their mothers and grandmothers before them, ringing in my head, telling me I'm crazy. But I refuse to cry, the way they did, whenever their husbands went stomping out the door. I stand in front of the mirror and force myself to keep my eyes wide open. Then I try to imagine what it would be like with a man who doesn't speak Greek. Yes, sometimes, when I look at my body in the mirror, I pretend I'm with a man who speaks some language I don't understand and who doesn't speak a word of Greek…

DIMITRI looks at her with a forced smile, trying to cover up the pain, and the string of the kite slips through his fingers.

DIMITRI   Poor Stella. If you made all that up just to hurt me—

STELLA   *(watching the kite fly away)* A hundred dollars. *(DIMITRI turns towards the exit. STELLA blocks his way.)* No. You can leave if you want, but don't play hurt.

DIMITRI   Stella…

STELLA   Leave if you want, but don't blame me! Anyway, nothing could be worse than your silence. Always the same damn silence. Don't you ever have fantasies?

DIMITRI   No, I'm just a peasant.

STELLA   Oh, go to hell! You and the whole lot of you! Bunch of hypocrites! *(She sits down. DIMITRI watches her.)* Is his lordship waiting for me to pack his suitcase for him?

DIMITRI   I can manage on my own, thanks.

STELLA   Right. "If you want something done well, do it yourself."

DIMITRI   That's true. Because whenever I've needed you—

            STELLA stares at him.

STELLA   When did you ever tell me you needed me?

DIMITRI   Even if I had told you, your heart was somewhere else. What good would it have done?

STELLA   You'll never know. *(She lies down.)*

DIMITRI   Stella... *(STELLA puts her arm over her eyes. She doesn't move throughout the following monologue. DIMITRI looks at her briefly, then:)* Stella... *(She doesn't move. He turns towards the exit.)* I bet that they would have admired me more if I'd fallen off the roof flying my kite than if I killed myself slaving in the store for them. *(He stops short, as if surprised, himself, by what he just said. He looks towards the edge of the roof. We can hear a fire engine siren racing by the house. Instinctively, DIMITRI takes out ANDREA's pack of cigarettes and moves slowly to the edge of the roof. He lights a cigarette, takes a puff, exhales.)* Aurora borealis. *(Another siren goes by. DIMITRI watches it disappear and speaks "in French.")* Beaucoup sirens today, eh? Like when *aeroplanas* came with *bombes*. Ou-ou-ou.... When I heard ou-ou—*vite* I put my head on *mamá*'s lap.

Mamá just do this. *(gesture of stroking his hair)* ...*moi* close eyes and *aeroplanas fini*... *(beat)* Close my eyes and everybody disappear, open them and everybody there again, just for me. Now.... Now I'm the one waiting for everybody to open their eyes so I can exist... *(He takes another puff.)* Ah! *C'est bon! C'est stoupide, mais c'est bon!* Oops! *(The smoke goes to his head and he staggers a bit at the edge of the roof.)* I was never afraid of heights when I was little. *Zamais tomber moi.* I could hear the heights calling me, like the sirens calling Odysseus. "Come, come. Don't go back to *Madame* Penelope. Come here." And I never strapped myself to my boat like Odysseus. When the heights called: "Come, Dimitri, come," I'd sing to myself. *Comme ça. (He leans over the side of the roof.)* Pam... pam.... *Moi ze sais beaucoup zansons.* Pam.... Pam.... No. *Moi comme papa de Mademoiselle Céline.* Now *moi* need cassette to remember words. *(He takes another puff.)* The last time I saw my father, it was nightime. Everyone in the house was asleep. Suddenly I heard my father calling me: "Dimitri, come on outside." Outside, my father said to me: "Look." "What?" "The chickens." "The chickens? You woke me up in the middle of the night so I could look at the chickens?" "Look, Dimitri, shut up and look!" I shut up and I looked. It wasn't really dark. Just beginning to get light. And the chickens were running around, like this... *(He imitates a hen pecking, cackling, and shaking her rear end.)* ...looking for something to eat. One minute. Two. Then suddenly: silence. The chickens stopped. *Comme ça. (frozen)* Like statues. Their eyes wide open. And they were all looking in the same direction, watching the huge orange rise on the horizon. And the rooster too. Five plump hens were standing right in front of him, *comme ça... (waving his rump)* ...but all the rooster could see was the sun rising behind the mountains. "Just imagine, Dimitri," my father said. "Imagine getting up every morning to greet the sun as if every day were the first time." *(He stares into the nothingness below him.) Stoupide, eh? Touzours rêver sozes impossibles....* Impossible dreams... *(He looks down into the street.)* Oh, there's her little prince, the artist. Talk, talk, talk away. Your days are numbered. Enjoy them.... And look at the other one listening to him, with a smile as big as the sun... I hope there'll always be a smile to light the way for him... *(Another siren goes by, STELLA lifts her head.)* Good. They've gone. Make sure your cigarette's out. No sense in burning their house down. *(He puts out his cigarette, looks up at the sky, takes a deep breath, and in preparation for his leap, he starts to spin, like a dervish starting to dance.)* One...! Two...!

> *STELLA has been watching him. She stands up and begins to talk to him "in French."*

STELLA   *Monsieur Dimitri! (DIMITRI stops spinning, dizzy. STELLA walks towards him, also dizzy from the wine.) Pas faire ça.* No count the stars. You get... ekzema.

DIMITRI   Huh?

STELLA   Never *un-deux-trois astra.*

DIMITRI   *Un-deux-trois astra?*

STELLA   *Zamais.* If you *un-deux-trois astra,* you have *beaucoup* ekzema on *dactylo.*

DIMITRI   If I count the stars, I'll get a rash on my fingers.

STELLA   That's what my grandmother told me.

DIMITRI   Did you ever get a rash?

STELLA   No. In Greece, impossible *un-deux-trois* all *astra* in sky.

DIMITRI   It's true. The sky was full of stars... *(They look up at the sky.)* Yeah... even the stars are rare now.

STELLA   Good. I can finally find out whether it's true, the story about the *ékzema. (She suddenly feels dizzy.)*

Ooops! *(She grabs onto DIMITRI.) Excouse. Moi pas voir…. Excouse-moi, Dimitri…*

DIMITRI   *(gently)* It's all right, it's all right.

He moves her away from the edge of the roof.

STELLA   We almost fall, eh? Our tsildren big now…. Nobody need us anymore.

DIMITRI   Sit down.

STELLA   Yes. You're right. No hurt *omoplates*. Better *un-deux-trois* on floor. Come.

DIMITRI doesn't move.

STELLA   *Toi peur,* eh? You afraid… count stars?

DIMITRI   Stella…

STELLA   *Toi* afraid *avoir* finger like pineapple!

DIMITRI   Stella, I wasn't counting—

STELLA   Shhh. *(She puts her finger on his lips.)* I know, my love. You weren't counting on staying. I'm just asking you to help me find all the stars. Then you can leave. There aren't that many… I know what we can do, I'll make you think you're already somewhere else. I'll count them in French. *(She looks up at the sky.)* It's true there aren't very many left. Just enough to make your hand a bit red. *(She points at the sky. The lights begin to go down.) Un astro…. Deux astra…*

DIMITRI   *Deux zétoiles.*

STELLA   *Deux zétoiles…. Trois zétoiles…. Quatre zétoiles…*

THE END

About the author

photo © Marie-Reine Mattera

Pan Bouyoucas came to Canada with his Greek parents in 1963. After studies in architecture, he obtained a BFA in film and theatre at Concordia University and worked a few years as a film critic. Since 1975 he has written in French seven novels, a collection of short stories, a book for children, a dozen radio dramas and stage plays, many of them translated into several languages. *From the Main to Mainstreet* (aka *Divided We Stand*), which he wrote in English, in 1989 for Montreal's Centaur Theatre, was the best selling show ever staged at Toronto's Canadian Stage Company. The recipient of many literary awards and nominations, in Canada and abroad, Bouyoucas is also a talented translator and the winner of the 2002 Quebec Writers Federation Prize for translation.

About the translator

Linda Gaboriau is a Montreal-based dramaturg and literary translator. Born in Boston, Massachusetts, Gaboriau moved to Montreal, Quebec in 1963 to pursue education in French Language and Literature at McGill University. She has worked as a freelance journalist for the CBC as well as the *Montreal Gazette*, and worked in Canadian and Quebecois theatre. Gaboriau has won awards for her translations of more than 70 plays and novels by Quebec writers, including many of the Quebec plays best known to English Canadian audiences. She is currently the Director of the Banff International Literary Translation Centre.